WHERE S
PR

Silence, the form of a melody
Alice Meynell: *To Silence*

Harmony, the silence of sound

Tibi silentium laus

WHERE SILENCE IS PRAISE

From the writings of A Carthusian

Translated from the French by A Monk of Parkminster

DARTON · LONGMAN + TODD

First published in 1960 by Darton, Longman and Todd

This edition published in 1997 by
Darton, Longman and Todd Ltd
1 Spencer Court
140–142 Wandsworth High Street
London SW18 4JJ

Imprimi potest: Fr Ferdinandus Prior Cartusiae In domo
Cartusiae.
Imprimatur: + Cyrillus Episcopus Southwarcensis
Nihil obstat: R D D Fogarty DD LCL, Censor deputatus.
Datum Southwarci die 28a aprilis 1960

ISBN 0–232–52184–0

A catalogue record for this book is available
from the British Library

Phototypeset by Intype London Ltd
Printed and bound in Great Britain by
Redwood Books, Trowbridge, Wiltshire

CONTENTS

∽∾

FOREWORD TO FIRST EDITION

∽∾

After *Silence Cartusien* and *Voix Cartusienne*, we offer
to the numerous and appreciative readers of those
works a selection of pages from the same pen, the
tone of which is slightly different. The following
extracts are drawn from notes which, it is hardly
necessary to say, were never intended in the writer's
mind for publication. The simple wisdom which
inspires them, however, would seem to justify us in
offering them to the public, and they will, we feel
sure, bring precious comfort to many souls.

The gathering together and choosing of these extracts has been a work of devotion and love. Once
again, as in *They Speak by Silences* by the same author,
they are not classified in any special order; but their
depth and clarity will, we trust, excuse anything
that may be wanting in their arbitrary arrangement.

These extracts have been translated from *Har-
monie Cartusienne*, published by the Benedictine
nuns of St Priscilla in Rome in 1954; together with
some hitherto unpublished notes taken after con-
versations with the author, which have been grouped
together under the general title of Counsels*.

St Hugh's Charterhouse
Parkminster, Sussex
Feast of All Saints, 1958

*In this edition 'Counsels' has been changed to 'Guidance'.

FOREWORD TO THIS EDITION

I was delighted when Darton, Longman and Todd decided to publish a new edition of *Where Silence is Praise*. It has received a thorough revision by a woman of keen literary sensibilities, and we feel sure it will be as valued by our generation as it was back in the sixties.

It is a worthy companion of *They Speak by Silences* which by its numerous editions is world-famous. Its author's French biography is titled *A Master of the Spiritual Life for our Time*. I pray this Cinderella of his works may quickly be found by all those who strive to love God.

St Hugh's Charterhouse
Parkminster, Sussex
October 1996

EXTRACTS FROM LETTERS

Realizing our being

∾∾

THERE IS ONLY ONE THING WE MUST ALL DO, and that is employ well the time and powers at our disposal. Only thus shall we realize our destiny, and that is the whole purpose of life.

The consciousness, realized as far as possible, of what we are and of what we do; the concentration of our whole being on the duty of the present moment: it is this that gives us our true value and develops it.

Once we have understood this and have the courage to live it; when, quietly and without undue strain and with just that effort of which we are capable at the time, we put all our strength into what we are doing, then we may be said to live fully.

Such a full life is not necessarily the life of a great man, but it is that of a human being, which is everything. To be little or great does not depend upon us, but to realize that being of which we are capable, moment by moment, does depend upon us, and it is this realization persevered in that makes us a complete person.

So carry on: you are on the right way. Give yourself wholly to what you are doing, without looking back or worrying over what the future will bring. Live just for today, for the present moment,

while it is yours to live . . . for so soon it will be
yours no longer.

Being ourselves

WE MUST NEVER FORGET THAT, IN SPITE OF ALL
our methods and all our efforts, we are and shall
always be different from others. It is foolish to
compare ourselves with others, and want to be like
them. When we do that, we are doing the very
thing that will make us apparently perfect, and yet
perfectly inadequate.

I do beg of you: do not try to be above or below
the golden mean. Try to be yourself, and to
realize the fullness of your own life, without
thinking that you are obliged to become a paragon
of perfection. Calmly weigh up your qualities and
defects, your inclinations and potentialities, and
with the means at your disposal and in the condition of mind and will, of aptitude and study, of
the ups and downs of life—according to all these
forces and circumstances, realize your talents fully.

It is not the result that counts, but the effort. I
may as well add right away that, taking a more
or less long view, the result will almost always
compensate for the effort. I would add, above all,
that, taking the highest and real point of view
(which is the true one, only unfortunately so few
realize it or appreciate it), the result always equals
the effort; and God, who moment by moment

keeps an account of our efforts, will one day strike a perfect balance between the two.

There is one aspect of this problem we sometimes forget, and that is, the diversity of our natures, and the corresponding effort required to develop and co-ordinate them according to that diversity. We are too apt to look at one another and make comparisons. We must take ourselves as we are. That is the starting point if we are to develop as much and as well as we can; but it will always be along the line of our personality, which is unique and must always remain so.

It must even become more and more unique. The more we are ourselves, the more we shall be different from everyone else.

Rise above yourself and things

∽∾

TRY TO RISE ABOVE YOURSELF AND THINGS.
Learn to control the wanderings of your thoughts,
and to turn them from one subject in order to
concentrate them upon another; to leave one task,
or to say No to a pleasure, even though it may be
a legitimate and a worthy one.

Keep your liberty in all that has not the right to
command you. Bend to him alone who is the
Master, and make your soul a taut canvas whereon
he can paint his image, which is Jesus.

Joy and pleasure

ᔌᔌ

Do not strive after a purely 'down to earth' aim in life, in which you may find pleasure, but follow a noble ideal which will give you joy.

To find pleasure is one thing; to be happy is another. Unfortunately for us, in this world the two do not always go hand in hand. Later on, when the two are one, it will be all right. Meanwhile, develop your mind and heart; discipline your will; be superior to all obstacles and pursue your way bravely towards your goal.

Detachment

༺༒༻

WE MUST NOT BE SLAVES EITHER OF TIME OR health; we cannot dispose of either as we will! If we thought of acting only when all the conditions were favourable, we would pass our lives doing nothing; or at least we would get out of life very little of what it can give us.

Go ahead! That is a phrase I like so much. Even if everything is far from perfect, we must learn to say it. And things will go ahead, since joy does not come from without or from circumstances. Its principal source is within us.

That is why faith is such a sure source of happiness, even now. The faithful who keep themselves in a state of grace, or who see that they return to it without delay whenever necessary, possess in their souls God who is infinite Goodness. And it is his presence that keeps them in peace. Troubles and disturbing events will always cause suffering; it is a law of life, and we cannot alter it.

We shall never banish suffering in our life, but we can forbid it entrance to our soul, or at any rate to the higher part of the soul. We are there, as it were, on a mountain, and we regard our troubles as the dweller upon the mountain contemplates the storm sweeping over the plain.

But we do not reach that height all at once; we

have to arrive at it by stages. The thousand and one petty annoyances that each day brings are our training. We must calmly watch them come and go. To want to avoid them all is impossible; to allow them to upset us is a weakness. There will always be some cloud on the horizon of our lives. But do not let any of these things stop you, or even affect you. In short: Go ahead!

Assimilation by the intellect

༄

SO FAR AS THE BODY IS CONCERNED, WE HAVE
to discover by experience, but without preoccupation, just how much and what kind of food we
need, and let all be governed by reason, without
taking any notice of our feelings. After some time,
and when it becomes second nature, we no longer
think about these things, and this becomes a precious form of detachment.

The same applies to our intellectual life. But
here note one thing especially. It is only what we
assimilate that nourishes us; all that is not assimi-
lated weighs us down and is a burden. This
assimilation is done, gradually and slowly, in the
depths of the subconscious mind. All that is not
immediately utilized is not lost, nor is it an encum-
brance. It lies dormant, and during this period of
apparent inertia, it undergoes mysterious develop-
ments which prepare it to play its particular part
in our lives later on.

Reading

∾

READING CAN BE PROFITABLE WITHOUT LEAVING any conscious trace in our memory. Here we must distinguish clearly between the memory and the mind. In order to fix something in our memory, we must concentrate on it; we note what enters and what remains in the memory. The intellect, on the other hand, allows ideas to penetrate without our necessarily being aware of the process. Some things, therefore, impress themselves upon the subconscious, which lies deeper than the conscious memory; and when we need them they come to the surface. Reading, then, is not a waste of time.

In order, however, to profit from our reading, we should read slowly. It is here above all that detachment is necessary. Usually we want to read too much, and to do too much. We want to cover ground; we strain ourselves, with the result that we get tired. All that we retain from our reading are vague notions, disconnected and lacking in clarity, cluttering up the mind instead of nourishing it, like a lot of undigested food. 'Little and good' is a sound maxim!

Little and good

∽∽

IN EVERYTHING WE SHOULD PREFER FORM TO
matter; quality to quantity; do little and that very
well, and strive always towards a high perfection,
which should always be progressive, so far as possible. Quality enriches, whereas quantity wearies
us to no purpose.

None the less, one should create one's own style
or way of doing things, and keep to it, always
developing oneself along the line of one's own
personality. Hence the need for that constant practice which makes perfect, and for widening and
enriching one's ideas. It is by this widening of our
mental horizon that we are fitted for the realization
of our ideals.

Relaxation

∾∾

SOME RELAXATION IS NECESSARY AFTER EFFORT. To know how to rest is a rare thing in this restless age of ours. We use up life, and spoil it, or at least lessen it as much by a want of moderation in what we do as by laziness. I would add, however, that I much prefer those who do too much to those who do too little!

In the case of intellectual work, it is the brain that gets tired, and it is the brain we must rest; and this we do by relaxing.

Rest, on the other hand, is not the same as idleness. The way to rest is not merely to cease working, unless one is obliged to through exhaustion, but to change one's work. Our new task will then bring into play powers, muscular or otherwise, which were not used, or very little used, in our preceding work. We rest by continuing to work, but varying the work.

Immobility

∾∾

THERE ARE TWO KINDS OF IMMOBILITY: TO BE pleased with oneself, and say: 'I have arrived, and that is good enough for me', and to be an idle person who says: 'It is too hard; I am going to stay where I am'. We must avoid both.

We must say to ourselves that we are far from the ideal which is our aim, and which will always be beyond our reach; but we should know that we are capable of striving towards that ideal, and can come always nearer to it. Nor need it surprise us that we have still a long climb ahead of us. It is those who realize that they have a long way to go, and who plod on, who succeed in the end.

What makes us human and worthy of the name, is keeping before our mind the ideal which shows us the perfection we are aiming at to the best of our ability, and perseverance in both will and effort to attain the summit we have in view.

Effort and success

꧁꧂

EFFORT MAKES US TRULY HUMAN, AND DIF-
ficulties brace us for the fight. Without
these, we can only call ourselves human shadows—
human in appearance only. So many are content
with the appearance! Do not be afraid to set your
compass, to face the issue, and to know how to
pass beyond the present moment (which is past
anyhow!) and tend more and more towards your
goal.

Obstacles? There will always be obstacles, and
we shall not always surmount them, either. Life
here below is not success; it is effort. Effort is the
test of our worth, and it is by effort alone that
we arrive at our goal. If success were a necessary
condition for our work, there would be any
number of things which we could not undertake,
but which we must undertake because they stand
for duty and for the ultimate good.

In any case, success is a word of wide meaning.
It can signify immediate realization, or easy and
quick results, which is what our present generation
has too eagerly sought; and it can also mean the
bringing into play of our whole strength in a constant struggle against the obstacles, both interior
and exterior, which rise up against it.

There have been very great people who have

been beaten in the battle of life, at least momentarily and often for long periods, who would never have achieved their stature but for their reverses.

Effort and method

ᗊᗊ

OUR TRAINING RECEIVES ITS VALUE AND produces its results in proportion to our effort, and in the measure of our method. Effort without method is fatiguing, and not very profitable; method without effort is valueless.

By that I do not mean that methods, any more than organizations, are perfect. Far from it! But while waiting for the necessary improvements, we must use the means at our disposal. Method is a means which makes effort easier, quicker in its results, and more fruitful. But it is only a means; it is not the end. If it makes for success, use it; if it does not, then don't! It is wisdom to know when to drop it when it no longer serves our purpose. Where it only partly serves our purpose, use it to that extent, and no more.

Effort and perseverance

❧

A RIGHT UNDERSTANDING OF THE STRUGGLE OF
life calls for perseverance. Not only because it is
always opening up new opportunities for our
effort, but because it represents an almost irresist-
ible force deep down in anyone who resumes, and
keeps up, the struggle.

You remember the definition of genius: 'Genius
is an infinite capacity for taking pains'. I believe
this to be an exaggeration myself, but only in the
phrasing. Deep down, the thought is correct. A
man who keeps pegging away and refuses to give
in until he has succeeded is a man who has in
himself more than we see.

Perseverance is the virtue which makes all effort
and method fruitful. And the condition for perseverance is a joyful courage. Sooner or later,
success is bound to follow.

Effort and waste

∾

WHEN OUR WORK BEGINS TO SLOW DOWN, WE must look for the reason. According to the reason, so will the remedy vary. If the cause is fatigue, then we must rest. If, on the other hand, it is laziness, then we must make the effort. Indeed, almost always, if our life is a well-regulated one, the best of all remedies is effort. But it is necessary to vary the effort. We rest from one task by undertaking another. A change is sufficient, since it is different powers which are being exercised.

Be that as it may, one must not dissipate one's energy by spreading it over too many objects. Otherwise we shall use ourselves up to no purpose, and the pleasure thus obtained will only be a superficial one and never a deep joy. Life is necessarily a unity: the more we are divided in ourselves, the more we resemble death, which is essentially separation. By running after everything, we possess nothing. By probing deep into one thing, we discover many other things. I do believe that if we could only reach the real depth of any one thing, we would find everything!

Effort consists in the control of our faculties. Instead of letting them run here and there, we concentrate them on the object we have in view. Effort, however, is aided by detachment, which is tranquillity of mind. We need to get rid of all preoccupation, all thoughts of success, all desire to have done with the struggle, all consideration of punishment or reward. We must turn ourselves wholly and quietly in the direction of our object, and concentrate on it the whole of our strength. In the same way, when we relax, we should relax whole-heartedly and not think about anything else.

To go 'all out' in whatever we undertake, using all our faculties, is the secret of all true development and of all true joy.

Calm courage

FACE LIFE BRAVELY AND FEARLESSLY. YET LET your courage be calm.

Courage without calmness is incomplete and imperfect. It is a promising bud, not yet open. Only when it has weathered seasonal storm and drought will it blossom and bear fruit.

Wishing and willing

∽∾

IF YOUR WILL HAS NOT NECESSARILY AN influence on others, it will have on your own actions, and that influence can be very great.

But note well the nature of that influence. The will is a master that does not act by itself; it needs servants and instruments. It has to set them going, and communicate to them its own will to act.

But servants are not always docile! In this case the intellect, the memory, the imagination and the external senses—the eye, the hand and so on—do not carry out the will's orders just when and how they are given. The servants have to be trained to submit, and for this the will has to form them, and this is a long and arduous undertaking. A decision taken one fine morning is not enough. The will only arrives at forming them after repeated efforts. These efforts make for habits, and the act follows, easily and happily, but only when habits have been formed.

What distinguishes wishing from real willing is this: the true will wants both the end and the means; mere wishing wants only the end. Simple desire is conditional: 'I would like to reach the end . . .' 'All right, go ahead!' 'But there is this difficulty . . . and that.'

And so mere wishing remains simply an unfulfilled desire—an intention, and nothing more.

Further, it is not a question of just saying or thinking; the essential thing is to act. Do thoroughly at every moment whatever it is you have to do. Then you will be strong, although you may not know that you are. By 'thoroughly' I mean with the firm conviction that you will arrive, and the determination to overcome, sooner or later, every difficulty.

Beauty

GOD IS AT THE DEEP CENTRE OF ALL THINGS,
and when we find him there we find eternal life.
Every creature gifted with reason has received light
to see in all created things both their own indi-
vidual beauty and that of the Supreme Being, from
whom they have received their being, and who
sustains them in it. With the light given us we
should see God in all things. Our gaze should pass
beyond the shadows of created things in order that
it may rest in the true Light hidden in beings
without reason, but discovered by those who have
reason. And with this Being we should make ourselves in harmony.

Breaking the husk

༺∽༻

ALL MATERIAL THINGS ARE A SOURCE OF BEAUTY and of enrichment.

It is not their fault that we do not profit by them more. The fault is ours entirely, in that we have not the courage to break the husk and seek the fruit.

Play of light

WITH YOU IN MIND, I WILL GAZE TOMORROW AT the sun setting on the whole range of colours with which the forest is decked for my restless eyes. Later, I will tell you of my impressions, if they are with me still.

Meanwhile, I reflect on the play of the divine Light in a soul which offers to it all its faculties and powers, all its tendencies and dispositions, all its movements and acts; and on the joy which we shall experience when we shall see all this interior world aglow, a spiritual forest more varied and more beautiful than the loveliest of earthly forests.

Travel

❧❧

TRAVEL DEVELOPS ALL OUR FACULTIES. WE
breathe a new and, generally speaking, a pure air,
which nourishes both body and soul. Our sensitive
nature is filled with images, with impressions and
memories, which enrich enormously our store of
knowledge. And this new knowledge is engraved
deeply on our minds, because it is new, and
because we travel precisely to have our eyes
opened.

Contract with our fellow travellers, and with the
people of the countries we visit, reveals to us
the diversity of human beings, but it reveals to
us also the common ground which we invariably
discover beneath these superficial differences. In
short, one acquires in a short time and during a
period of relaxation, what months of study could
not give, or not in the same way.

You have made a lot of acquaintances; have you
made any friends? Have you made contact with
the more intimate life of all the places you have
visited? Have you penetrated their outward
appearances, perceived the details of their lines,
observed their hues, the ever-changing shadows of
which they are composed? Have you divined the
psychology of the 'race' which inhabits them?

Have you brought back with you a treasure all your own?

Friendship's threshold

∽∽

IF YOU WOULD CROSS FRIENDSHIP'S THRESHOLD, do not forget that the primary and essential condition is renunciation: that is to say, perfect disinterestedness in the search for your friend's good, his interests, his happiness, all that is to his advantage. Remember also that there is no such thing as an ideal friendship, nor is it necessary. Life never gives us all that we hope for, and we must face life as we find it. The fact is we all have faults, many more than we think, and they cause others suffering. Nevertheless, in spite of these faults, we must love one another; and if we love one another truly, we shall try to correct these faults in our friends. It is on this understanding that friendship merits its name and plays its part. Otherwise, it remains merely companionship.

There is no doubt that true friendships have existed, and always will exist. But I believe that they are very rare, the more so perhaps these days than formerly. For friendship is the very opposite of the self-centredness which is so common. The egoist thinks only of himself; a friend, on the contrary, gives his whole thought and love to his friend, so that they may become one.

When circumstances permit, one must cross this threshold and not be afraid. Its gains far outweigh its losses. So take no notice of all the weaknesses and faults which are inseparable from life, and you will be immeasurably the gainer.

Life a synthesis

∽∾

LIFE IS A SYNTHESIS WHICH DISINTEGRATES when we try to analyse it in order to grasp it. Be content to live it.

You know the secret. Here it is in three words:

> *God is Love.*
> *We . . . believe the love God has for us.*
> *Everyone who believes in me has life.*

'Love' (charity): love is the origin of everything. 'Life': life is the goal of everything. 'We believe': in the faith Love unites us.

Make that *we believe* your own, and act more and more on it: that is life.

On God's level

∽∽

IT IS A LAW OF LIFE THAT WE ARE SLOWLY transformed by those with whom we are brought into contact. Love makes like. Love causes us to go out of ourselves and live in those we love. It moves us to make their thoughts and feelings our own, to share in their lives, and so become one with them. Thus admiration invites imitation. Almost irresistibly we feel impelled to imitate all that appears to us good and beautiful; we set it up as a model that we would copy.

Religion is such a contact. It creates ties which bind God and the believer. If our god is matter, we become material; if it is something beneath us, we are lowered. Union is only possible when two beings approach and meet on a common level.

The sole Good

∽∿∽

WE HAVE BEEN REDEEMED BY GOD. THAT IS
the great gift of life. For there is only one Good,
namely God. And life has only one blessing to
give us, and that is communication with him and
participation in his life. We exist only by him; we
only live when united to him. Sin is death, because
it separates us from him. Redemption gives us
back life, since it permits and enables that reunion.
And that reunion should be eternal, and should
be a final union, for it consists in a unity which
nothing but sin can break.

The Indefinable

∽∾

HAS ANYONE EVER TOLD US WHAT GOD IS?
No—only what he is not! In a sense, that is all one
can say about him. But we must not complain; on
the contrary, we should be glad for his sake, for
to define anything is to set bounds to it, and God
has no bounds. He is infinite. That thought ought
to make us rejoice, and in all eternity it will, in
fact, overwhelm us with joy. We shall be able to
contemplate him unendingly, and unendingly we
shall discover in him fresh perfections and beauty,
and unendingly he will appear to us as unknown,
as unfathomable and as desirable, as though the
eye of our soul, opened wide by the light of
Heaven, rested upon him for the first time.

God is. That is all he is. Every created being is
something 'particular'. It is not only a being that
exists, but 'such and such' a being. It has a name
and form which distinguish it from everything else.
Its form is constituted by its limits, by the lines
which denote where it ends.

God, on the other hand, is a Being of whom,
when one has said 'He is', one has said all. Having
said that, one distinguishes him from everything
else. Being is his form; Being is his Name. It is
the Name he gave himself: *I am he who is.*

All other beings are 'particular' beings. He—he

is: nothing more. He is Being Itself. If I add to this Name, no matter how tiny a thing, I define him; I give him limits; I limit him.

This is the unique greatness of God, which places him beyond everything; different from everything else; on heights where there is room for him alone, where he dwells alone.

Magnificat

~~~

MAGNIFICAT . . . HOW CAN ONE MAGNIFY GOD?
He is infinite greatness, and one cannot add to the
infinite. One cannot alter and enlarge the limits of
someone who has no limits.

One must not be surprised at these apparent
contradictions when we speak of God. Our human
language comes from something created; it is
made to express things that are circumscribed. In
face of the infinite, our stutterings tremble like
human shoulders bent under an impossible load.

Yet Our Lady uses this vehicle which we find so
inadequate. Her thought is far vaster than the
words that convey it.

Try hard to catch something of that immense
thought.

True knowledge of God

∽∽

THE KNOWLEDGE AND UNDERSTANDING OF
God, which is the reward of those who put into
practice what they believe, and whose love is
equally genuine, alone assures salvation.

To know, love and serve God: this is life, and this
is salvation. To know and love—yes, that is good,
and it is necessary. But it is not enough. We must
also act. When we shall find ourselves face to face
with God, he will not be content merely with our
thoughts and feelings; he will ask us: 'What have
you done for love of me?' There are many people
who, having spoken wonderful things about him,
will appear empty-handed, simply because their
works have not corresponded with their words.

To understand God we must understand that.
God himself was not content with just thinking
about doing us good, or merely desiring it; he
really has given us our being, our life, as well as
all that is necessary to keep us in being. More, he
has truly given us his divine Son. The Passion of
Our Lord, the Holy Eucharist—these are not just
idle dreams, they are realities. The gift of oneself,
by which we must respond to the gifts of God,
this, too, must be a reality. We are bound to give
ourselves as he gives himself: that is to say, not
only in words but in deeds.

Living friendship

∽∾∽

REAL FRIENDSHIP IS VERY RARE, EXTREMELY rare in history, for it calls for natures that are already very lofty, and it elevates them still more.

Friendship with Jesus, however, is of a far more exquisite quality, and it brings to souls blessings that are infinitely superior. It consecrates friendships that are purely natural, and raises them up and endows them with a supernatural quality. That is why we should cultivate both at the same time.

Unfortunately, this second friendship is difficult, because the object of our love is not such as comes within the scope of our senses, and our relations with Jesus are bound to follow the way of spiritual things. These make little impression on us, just because they do not appeal to our senses. One needs time to understand the things of the soul, and to experience the relations that souls can have with one another. How often do we not say: 'I do not forget you; you are always in my thoughts'. But do we reflect on the deep reality that lies beneath our words?

We do not understand, or rather we do not realize, that when two souls are united, they do not lie side by side like two bodies; they are really each in the other. And this is the principle of all love union, and in particular of that friendship which is the highest form of that union. Two friends become one, because their minds and their hearts are in perfect harmony, in the worship of the same truth and in the love of the same good. That community of love—note the word 'community' which means 'common-unity' and is very significant—increases our life twofold, and makes our being greater with all the greatness of the life of the one we love. That is how, when we love God and when we enter into these relations of friendship with him, our life takes on a wideness which is measureless, and becomes eternal life.

Love's exchanges

∾∾

THERE IS NO NEED TO WAIT FOR THAT KNOW-ledge which is the result of study before acting in the region of our relations with God. Religion is belief: but above all, it is practice. It is not knowledge.

It is a mutual exchange of love, and it is in this exchange that God reveals himself. He reveals himself in the measure in which we love him, not according to our learning, even in the matter of our religion.

It is not necessary to know precisely all the perfections of God, nor to be able to expound eloquently all the arguments which prove his existence. How many souls pass the whole of their lives without knowing these things, and yet how profound is their knowledge of him, how warm their fervour, and how intensely real their relations with him.

These souls look upon God as a Father, who is unceasingly communicating to them his thoughts and desires, and it is by these thoughts and desires they live. He becomes, as it were, their very soul and their innermost life. His Spirit abides in the depths of their spirit, enlightening, encouraging and directing all the inner resources that they possess.

41

And they love the Father, and hold converse with him. They share with him their joys and their sorrows, and he is the secret confidant of all their hours. He is there, in the depth of their soul, waiting to receive them into his intimate dwelling-place the moment they turn to him. They recognize him, and they know that it is he who is calling them, whenever an interior voice invites them to think of him. Their minds meet inevitably, and thus they enter into a relationship at once living, continuous, and full of delight—a relationship between the soul and its divine Guest, which grows in intensity.

The commandments of God

∽∽

A STATUE CARVED IN A ROCK WILL LAST AS LONG as the rock itself: it has the same stability. The commandments of God are carved in the immovable rock of Truth and Justice, and this rock is God. Nothing can break them or threaten their solidity. Like the line of the shadow cast by the sun upon the ground, we can side-step them but we cannot alter them. We may swerve from our duty, but we cannot get rid of it. Our duty remains our duty, in spite of all our violations of it; and the device is there for those who violate it to read: 'This is what is true; what is just; what is good'.

Time, which consumes most things, cannot touch the commandments. The passing of time makes no difference to them, and down the long ages they retain their vigour and their obligation.

The commandments of God, then, no less than his mercies, are worthy of being sung by the faithful.* To our observance of them we should add our praise; practising them, we should admire and love them. Or, better, observe them with love, reflecting while doing so on the joy of the One

*Cf. Ps. 88:1 (Vulgate): *Misericordias Domini in aeternum cantabo . . . The mercies of the Lord I will sing for ever.*

who in love has prescribed them, and thus return love for love.

Happy those souls who know how to recognize in the commandments of God the tenderness of a Father. For them, obedience is easy and immeasurably profitable. Their very duties, instead of weighing them down, give them wings; their very efforts, instead of overwhelming them, lift them up and carry them up to heaven.

Essential happiness

∾∾

WHAT DO I UNDERSTAND BY ETERNITY? I DO NOT
understand it. The idea of eternity is like so many
other ideas. The idea does not represent the reality,
but merely the impression it makes; the negative
of it. I can only visualize things which begin and
end. These are the only things I can understand
and give a name to. The rest I can only define by
excluding all idea of ending, of measure or time.
And so I speak of the *in*finite, the *im*mense, the
eternal.

But that does not tell me what the infinite or
the eternal is; it simply tells me what it is not. It
is the same with the word 'day'. Day is not just
the disappearance of darkness (that is, something
purely negative) but above all the coming of light
(something positive). What is there either positive
or negative about the idea of eternity; or in the
reality itself? Philosophers have done their best to
elucidate it, and this is what they tell us.

When I speak of eternity, I at once negate all
beginning and all end. So far negation. At the
same time, I affirm that the reality, which has
never begun and will never end, possesses fully all
the being of which it is capable; has always pos-
sessed it, and will always possess it. That is to say,
it is changeless. There you have affirmation. The

idea of eternity is, therefore, a secondary idea derived from the idea of changelessness.

Created beings are in movement because they do not possess the fullness of their being; they have to develop in order to achieve it. They are in movement in order to arrive. They are becoming; as yet they *are not*. They are moving towards their end, because they have not yet reached it. When they have reached it, they will cease to move, and they will rest in that end. Eternity, for them, is thus rest in the full possession of all the being of which they are capable.

Essential suffering—I am not saying the suffering we feel most in this life—is being not united to the One who is the fullness of Being, infinite Being. Essential happiness is to be united to him for ever.

Now we have been given a certain time in order to move towards and be united to God; this is the transitional time of life. Then, having once made our choice, we shall enter upon a time which is 'still', and this we call eternity. If, on entering this time we have achieved union with infinite Being, then we shall want for nothing more, and we shall be happy. And as that Being is immutable, and has no changeable time, we also shall be unchangeably and eternally happy. If, on the other hand, we are separated from that fullness of Being, we shall lack everything, and we shall no longer be able to possess him, since all movement will have ceased. And we shall suffer accordingly.

Deep down, all rests upon two concepts: on the one hand, that of happiness (which is possession) and evil (which is privation); on the other, that of immutability, which is the sole prerogative of the *Being who is*; whilst the being who has not yet arrived at his fulfilment must change in order to do so and arrive at his goal. In other words, he is in motion.

One can well understand how every created being is in movement, because they have not their end in themselves, and must move, therefore, in order to reach that end. Unfortunately, we deceive ourselves as to our end. We run after things that are not our end, which change and are transitory like ourselves, and which are constantly eluding us, leaving our hearts empty.

Spiritual blindness

༄

IN EVERY REDEEMED SOUL MIRACLES OF GRACE have been accomplished. Baptism has freed us from bondage, while the sacrament of penance liberates us again when we fall back into it.

But these wonders are purely spiritual, and make no impression on us, so profoundly are we under the spell of the senses. We are like the blind, confronted with the loveliest of scenes. We say: 'It is nothing', whereas what we ought to say is: 'I see nothing, because I lack the necessary organs of vision'.

Let us ask God to give them to us, because there is nothing so beautiful and so delightful as the inward scenes and hidden mysteries of the life of the spirit.

Passions which lessen us

❦

WE SHOULD BE GLAD TO BE AWARE OF THE dangers of those desires to which we give way, for they lessen our moral stature. I am referring to what we call passion.

Now passion is a force or power which is indispensable if we are to be human. But it must be canalized and not allowed to run wild. That does not mean for a moment that our sensitive nature must be crushed, but it does mean that it must be reduced to order, which is quite another matter. In these days, people indulge it wildly for a few years, and then, to all intents and purposes, suppress it altogether for the rest of their lives. That is why there are so many cases in the world today of unbalanced people who lack both heart and feelings.

Properly controlled, our sensitive nature develops quietly, at an even pace, and, slowly brought under the influence of reason and faith, attains that perfect balance which makes for genius. We have no idea of the extent of the influence of heroic acts accomplished at twenty, which constitute a reserve of energy most precious for the future. At thirty, these acts become difficult; at forty, almost impossible. After that, there is nothing to do but resign ourselves to the inevitable decline.

By the practice of virtue, we can fashion for ourselves a soul free to rise superior to things. But once we give way to passion, it is the beast which dominates the mind, and man is debased. Be on your guard against anything that is likely to carry you off your feet. That is the danger of the passions. They grasp at everything; they must have the monopoly; they allow no rivals. The result is an intense concentration which is actually their strength, but it is a false strength, because their energy is not centred around a reality worthy of them.

In speaking of passion, one must distinguish. Unfortunately we have lost the habit of doing so, in this age of insufficient formation and narrow ideas. In itself passion is neither good nor bad; its value is that of the object which provokes it. When we desire inordinately something which is less than ourselves, we become less; when it is something bigger, we become greater. When it is God, we become like God. This is because we make the object of our passion the principle of our life, and starting from that principle build up a life which is that of the object towards which we tend, enriched by ours, but ours absorbed by the object and becoming its own.

This is the explanation of the destroyed equilibrium brought about by original sin. Human beings were made for God, and placed in his presence, with the intention that they should find their fulfilment and happiness in God. Satan drew their attention away from God to creatures, and humankind believed him. They thus fell from the divine height where they had been placed to this level, human and created. And we see what human nature is when it is no longer upheld by God and uplifted by him.

A saint is one who turns back to God, and only sees and desires creatures in him and for him; just as God himself sees and wills the creature. Little by little, step by step, the saint climbs up, not without effort or slipping, sometimes even falling; but always getting up again and continuing the climb, in spite of everything, until he reaches the height from which we fell.

The centre of our lives

❧

OUR MODEL IS JESUS. AND THAT MEANS COM-
plete contempt for all that fallen nature has preferred to God; and so, indifference and
detachment. For the follower of Christ, the goods
of this world are not his master; he is not dominated by them. When, in the normal course of
things, they come his way, he accepts them; when
they do not, he does without them. He is superior
to them—above them. His life has its source higher
than these things; it has its centre in God, who
alone suffices for him, and is his sole good.

I need hardly remind you that this unique centre
does not exclude other affections and activities; on
the contrary, it includes them. The supernatural
life is not a narrow and poor life; it is essentially
wide and rich. It brings all within its scope, but
all in order, everything in its place. It takes to
itself all our faculties and all our senses, and
embraces in its sweep all that we do, all that we
think, all that we love, and directs the whole
towards the end which is the true good, and to
him who is its Source.

Hence both its complexity and its unity. And
this, because its term is most high; indeed, the
Infinite. And so I come back to what I said before:
passion has the value which its object imparts to it.

If that object is the Infinite, it will give to existence an infinite value and plenitude.

Why we suffer

∽

WE ARE NOT FOND OF SUFFERING, AND, IN ONE
sense, we are right. We are made for happiness,
and it should be the dream of our hearts, the
aim of our existence. We are not wrong to seek
happiness, but we are wrong to seek it along wrong
paths.

Where are we to find it? In God alone. He is
that mysterious Reality for whom we long in all
that we desire, in all that we do. He hides himself
in the depth of all created things, from which we
ask happiness, and which cannot give it to us.
They are the veil which hides the infinite beauty
of his Face, and we suffer because we stop at that
veil, instead of passing beyond it. When we pass
beyond the veil and meet the Reality which is
behind it all, then are we consoled, and our joy
is full.

Love's pursuit

∽∾

GOD HAD GIVEN TO THE HUMAN CREATURE
every possible gift. He had called him to share in
his own divine life. By a privilege, the magnitude
of which will only be revealed to us in heaven,
man was able to know God as God knows himself,
and to love him as he loves himself. To his mind
God had given a higher light by which he could
contemplate Truth itself, and in his heart a spark
of that infinite charity by which he could love the
sovereign Good, and be united to him and possess
him.

And man lost that sublime crown which gave
him a place in heaven, and was the richest portion
of that treasure of being which was God's gift to
him. And he found himself in the dust and in need,
crouched upon the earth that he had preferred to
God, despoiled of his soul's divine adornment.

In that misery, the eyes of infinite Love followed
him, drew him out of that misery and gave him
back his beauty and his splendour. Humankind
was the King's daughter, and the Son of God
came to restore in her the image of the Father. He
washed away her stains, bathed her in his Precious
Blood, traced anew in her the effaced traits of
the divine Face. He remade her in the image and
likeness of infinite Beauty. Only then was she able

to shake herself free of that earth which is poverty indeed; only then did she recover her right to her Father's home: an inheritance which is the abode of the spirits of the just, the high heaven itself where God dwells, the kingdom of the Father.

The kingdom of God

∽∽

JESUS SAID: *THE KINGDOM OF GOD IS WITHIN you.* That is to say, in that deep and mysterious part of the soul we call the centre, the innermost chamber, and, again, the apex of the soul. It is the temple, the sanctuary, the altar that the Father chose as his dwelling-place on the day of our baptism, and it is there he bids us join him. And we respond to that invitation when we enter into recollection.

Like bees, our faculties come and go ceaselessly, settling and feeding upon any object that presents itself to them. These objects are good, but they are not the ultimate good. They are from God, but they are not God. They lead us to him; they make us think of him, but they do not replace him. Our faculties must return to the hive, and bring to the divine Majesty who dwells there all the wealth that they have gathered. It is there the honey is made. They enter there by recollection, and there they reassemble and bring together the fruits they have collected, offering them to their Creator.

Then he, in turn, brings to bear on these fruits of the soul—its memories and images, its thoughts and feelings, its desires, fears and hopes—the light of the heavenly radiance which transforms them and makes them resplendent in beauty. The fruits of the soul, offered to God by the soul, thus become his fruits and the soul's.

Recollected within herself, the soul, laden with her treasures, joins the Father in the silent sanctuary wherein he dwells, and takes up her abode with him. She is the Queen of this interior kingdom, of which she has chosen him as King. He invites her to share his throne, and they enter into those ineffable relationships which we try to imagine and express in words, but the reality of which surpasses inexpressibly all human language in depth and charm.

Dawn of the eternal day

∽∾

PROMPTED BY THE HOLY SPIRIT, THE SOUL begins to see as he sees, to judge as he judges, to love as he loves. He is the Master within: the soul, so to speak, of the soul, the high radiance revealing the passing things of earth in their true light, so much so that the soul chooses the eternal realities. Amidst the shadows which original sin has spread in and around the soul, that eternal splendour is its Guide, filling it with security and joy. In this heavenly Light, the soul recognizes the divine Guide who leads her unfailingly to her true home.

Henceforth, even the shadows become light. Passing things, instead of holding back the soul, remind her of the things which do not pass away. The soul now sees the former in the light of that higher radiance, recognizing in them the hand of the Master whom alone she loves. She thanks him and praises him in these wonders which reflect him; and she praises him within herself, where he diffuses that ever-blessed Light, which is himself.

Such is truly the dawn of day, the eternal day; the rising of the Sun of Justice within the soul. As nature awakens and appears to come to life again with each dawn; as the truths of the spirit become luminous in the measure in which one discovers them, so the soul, enlightened by God, sees herself and all things in a new radiance.

Delight and joy

ഗ്ഗ

GOD IS THE DELIGHT AND JOY OF THE SOUL. HE is behind all delight and all true joy. He is their secret soul and the source of their attractiveness.

We are only moved by things in so far as they reflect the divine within them. That is why created things leave us so empty and unsatisfied, for they contain only the merest fraction of the infinite, whereas we are made for the whole.

The only true greatness

∽∽

TRUE GREATNESS AND THE ONLY REAL BEAUTY come from our perfect correspondence with the divine plan. The perfection of a fir tree is not the same as that of an oak; nor the beauty of a rose that of a violet.

Each being has its own perfection. In the realization of each of these perfections consists the beauty of the universe. And in the realization of our own perfection we who are gifted with reason find our joy.

Reverential love

∽∽

ONE MUST CONTEMPLATE THE GREATNESS OF God in order to understand and experience his love; to know the Lord, the supreme Master, in order to love the Father with a love unchanging and deep, which becomes neither familiarity nor irreverence. The liveliest transports of love are born of these thoughts: this goodness so compassionate is that of the infinite Being; that love, that understanding, those exchanges of love, that life with God and in him—he alone can give them. Without him, we should possess nothing; without him we should be nothing.

∽∾

PRAISE DOES NOT EXCLUDE PETITION. GOD wants to be praised. He wants that, in the face of his greatness, the first cry of the soul should be one of admiration. But he loves also that we should realize our weakness, and tell him of our needs. In the last resort, the greatest thing about him is his goodness. He is the 'good' God: the Being who gives himself, communicates himself, pours out on others, and that in an unlimited degree, his treasures and his joy.

In begging him for further favours, we thereby recognize those he has already given us. To appeal to his goodness is the way to the divine Heart.

Peace of a heart that 'showeth mercy'

∽∾

IN ORDER TO BE TOUCHED BY THE SUFFERINGS of others, we must first of all overcome our own self-love, and take our passions in hand.

The heart that 'showeth mercy',* which has pity for all frailty and the generosity to come to its aid, will experience a peace which does not change, a calm without cloud—almost, one might say, a participation in the divine unchangeableness.

*Cf. Ps. 111:5 (Vulgate): *Jucundus homo qui miseretur et commodat . . . Acceptable is the man that showeth mercy.*

Unclouded joy

∽∾

THE GREATEST JOY, IF IT CAN COME TO AN END, is not perfect joy. The fear of losing it is a perpetual menace, and casts thereon its shadow. *The right-eous will never be moved . . . They are not afraid of evil tidings.* The joy of the just knows not this shadow; its region is beyond all passing clouds, for its source is God, who knows no change.

It is in God that the just live. Their abode is the divine Mind.* They dwell there continuously. They see God as an infinitely loving Father in the depth of their soul. Their faith reveals that pres-ence and recalls to them that love. They believe that at every instant this Father is communicating to them his own Spirit, his own life. They turn away from all created things in order to welcome him. They make every effort to turn to the Father, even as the Father is unceasingly turned towards them. They place their mind in God's mind, and in that union find a stability which is even now a foretaste of eternal life.

At these heights evil does not touch them. They are in God; they are in their supreme Good.

*Cf. Wisdom 5: 16 (Vulgate): *Cogitatio illorum apud Altissimum . . . The reward of the just is with the Lord, and the care of them with the most High.*

Others may speak of them, think of them, do what they will with them: their soul dominates and despises these vain attacks of a world which no longer counts with them. They leave the creature—inviting him to come out of himself—for the Creator, who bids them be still and dwell with him in his heart. That place where now they love to dwell is a place to which neither the world nor the devil has access. It is the abode of the Father, the innermost sanctuary where the Father gives himself to those who seek him alone. It is the sacred retreat, where the life of heaven already begins to take form here below.

Renunciation which sets us free

～

SACRIFICE AND RENUNCIATION ALLOW US TO
give ourselves to God. They sever the human and
created ties which hold back the soul. They set
the soul free and permit it to wing its way towards
those high regions where we find peace.

Breaking that does not separate

ᔕᔐ

WE HAVE ALL OF US AT SOME TIME BROKEN, more or less, the hearts of those we love most in the world; and we, too, have had our hearts broken in the same way. Only those who have had the direction of souls know how much we must love them to cause them suffering. Yet we must do so, if we are to lead them to the heavenly embrace of the divine Saviour on the Cross.

The love of God does not mean that we may not have our legitimate affections. It only seems to do so. When the love of God takes possession of a soul and carries it away with him far from the hearth so beloved, it does not touch our attachment to our home and our loved ones there. We know that behind the walls of a cloister and in the silence of a cell, in confiding to God the care of making known to them our affection and of realizing in their regard the dreams of our love, we do far more for them than our actual presence could have accomplished.

Suffering we can bear

∽∽

ALL LOVE IS BORN OF THE LOVE OF THE FATHER
and of the Son. With Jesus, charity and peace met
again on earth, and their first-born, joy, flourished
anew in souls rejuvenated and consoled.

May all our hours of sacrifice find their fulfilment in union with the sacrifice of our Leader,
and draw from that union the secret and rapturous
joy of the gift of self. No trial is too heavy to be
borne, once we possess the hope of eventual union
with infinite Joy. All sorrow lit up by the divine
sorrow takes on an aspect of joy, and the greatest
suffering then becomes the greatest happiness.

Difficulties

❧

YOU HAVE DONE WELL TO EXPOSE YOUR DIFFI-
culties. By doing so, you have freed your soul, and
that is already something. Often that is all we can
do in this life, and we must be content with that.
It is good to know how to do so from time to time.

Do not be too distressed over your shortcomings, nor with the difficulty you experience in
overcoming them. I have a feeling that the imperfections you speak of are nothing more than those
miseries of which someone has said that if we had
none to begin with, we should lose no time in
'buying' them ... Since we are living in hard
times, here at least is something you can purchase
over the counter!

Examine yourself from time to time, but quietly
and with liberty of spirit, to see whether there is
not some special point on which God is asking
you to make an effort which so far you have
refused him. If there is, try to correct yourself on
that point; if there is not, remain at peace and
continue to accept not being today what you will
have to be tomorrow. Life is a growth, slow and
imperceptible. We will not hurry matters by constantly watching the progress we are making. You
have within you an interior Master, who will tell
you what to do and what not to do. Be guided by

him. Be as faithful as you can to the indications he gives you, and wait with confidence and calm the realization of a design of love which he will bring about, if you do not hinder him, and which he wants to bring to a happy consummation even more than you.

I am glad to hear that you are going on well; above all that you are at peace. The enthusiasm that you say you lack is not really necessary: it is a luxury! When God gives it, it is a great help, but when he withholds it, what he gives instead is quite sufficient. You will accustom yourself little by little to be content with what God sends, and to draw profit from it. The effort called for here and now has this object in view, and it will help you to advance along his way much quicker than you think.

Life is in movement

∽∾

IT IS GOOD THAT YOU ARE INTERESTED IN ALL these questions . . . One has to study them for a long time before they become a reality. For us, for whom study is a duty, it is rare that we realize them without having studied them. Study shows that we really love them, and when that is so, God sooner or later gives us the grace to live them. Do not forget that 'sooner or later'; do not be in a hurry. The best way to make progress in a question like this of life, is to go slowly; or, better, to keep in step with God, who is never in a hurry. Life is a journey. Provided we keep going, all is well. What God cannot tolerate—what is, indeed, intolerable—are those stationary souls who are either inert by nature, or who persuade themselves that they have reached the summit, and that there is nothing more for them. Train those committed to your charge along those lines, and teach them to keep steadily moving. *Vita in motu* . . . life is in movement.

Life is a movement

∽∽

IT IS NOT NECESSARY THAT OUR REPRODUCTION
of Jesus should be perfect today, nor even
tomorrow . . . It is only necessary that we should
tend towards that perfection; that we should never
give up striving and wanting to strive. So long as
we are in this world, life is a movement towards
its Source. After, that is in the next world, it will
be a movement in that Source. Our failings are
not an obstacle. The real obstacle is our laziness
which puts up with our defects and makes no
effort to get rid of them.

Abandonment

∽∾

I AM NOT SURPRISED THAT YOU FIND DE Caussade's *Abandonment to Divine Providence* a help. It is an excellent work, and one cannot read it too much or meditate on it enough. I have one fault to find with it, however; not so much with the author himself, as with the way in which he presents the development of the spiritual life. He speaks so little of Our Lord. He keeps us always in the presence of the divine perfections. Such a doctrine leads to the prayer of quiet, acquired or infused. That is all right, but it is not the end. Our Lord is indispensable if the soul is to reach the supreme heights of true abandonment, which is the apex of union with God. Without him, we can remain in the presence of a Master, but union with God of necessity means being in the presence of a Father. And it is Jesus, the Son made man, who puts us there.

Pray very much for the poor world, which is more and more heading for the abyss . . . but the good God is waiting for it at the bottom of the abyss.

Making decisions

∾∾

I HAVE NOTHING SPECIAL TO ADD AS REGARDS your first question. In God's good time, he himself will provide the answer, and you will be amazed and delighted at his solution, which will quite possibly be the very opposite of what you imagine now. God gives you now the grace to study the question and work out the answer. Later on he will give you the grace to act. Nothing is more important in life than to know how to wait on God, and to bring what we are doing into line with what he wants, moment by moment.

Times of great stress are, generally speaking, not the times to make decisions. We do not see clearly enough; we know not what the morrow will bring; indeed, we barely know the message of today. Await the calm, and the light that the calm brings. It is an effort imposed on our too eager zeal, which is always one of the most redoubtable enemies of supernatural activity. Yet it is precisely in that effort that God finds his glory.

Draw much profit from your contacts with those with whom you are in touch by word or letter. There is a great deal to be learned and gained thereby. You will see how, and how much, God is at work; but also, alas! how, and how little, we respond to his advances. Souls that are truly docile and persevering are very rare.

The Divine Master

∽∾

MANY QUESTIONS APPEAR VERY COMPLICATED when considered in theory, but on the practical plane everything becomes clear and simple. This is especially the case if we can reduce all to Jesus himself, not merely his doctrine, his Gospel, his Church, his public life, but his Person: that divine and human unity so completely full, perfect and harmonious, in which all his perfections are so wonderfully merged that one no longer notices them; where his greatness is so simple and his simplicity so great; where there are so many perspectives and horizons that the more one contemplates them, the more one advances and the more one discovers to admire, to love and to imitate; where in the end we find Someone who loves us, who gives himself to us, and becomes our father, our mother, our brother, sister, friend and spouse—he himself has said it—and much more still, for our words remain at an infinite distance from that boundless Reality. March as long as you like, and as rapidly as you like, and you will still have far to go, and you will still want, more and more, to go . . . *Those who drink of me will thirst for more.*

Continue, then, to apply yourself ever more deeply to the study of Our Lord, especially as you feel drawn that way. He himself is the great Source from whom everything flows. We know nothing truly, we comprehend nothing, unless we know him. He is the true Light that lightens and explains everything.*

*Cf. John 1:9 (Vulgate): *Erat lux vera, quae illuminat omnem hominem venientem in hunc mundum* . . . *That was the true light, which enlighteneth every man that cometh into the world.*

GUIDANCE

God alone

〜✄〜

BE CALM, INFINITELY CALM, BOTH IN SOUL AND in body. Do not attempt too much, but what you do, do well and gently. Quality first, but good quality. Follow grace in souls; take its step. It is *adagio*; often *adagissimo*, but very sure. Forget yourself completely—time, studies, health, reputation . . . Give yourself utterly, without counting the cost, without reserve, without thought of yourself. God alone!

Daily upsets

∽∾

WE KNOW THAT ALL THINGS WORK TOGETHER *for good for those who love God.* To those with good will: that is to say, those who, submitting and making over their reason and will to the Holy Spirit and allowing themselves to be guided by him, invariably arrive at that perfection willed for them by God. That does not mean that we can sit with our arms folded and leave it all to him. On the contrary, we must make use of all that divine Providence sends us: reverses, falls even; bearing always in mind the good that the Holy Spirit wants to draw from these things. Given that disposition, the Holy Spirit will never be absent. He also makes use of reverses to correct our faults and set us on our way again. Use everything, then, with this end in view; in all weathers, keep your compass pointing to God; make him your aim.

The will

ᔕᔕ

THE WILL IS A MASTER THAT HAS, IN THEORY, the ordering of everything, but, in fact, the full control of nothing. It becomes 'will' when it seeks to claim its 'rights'; to acquire mastery over the passions and feelings. It is 'good' when this is done according to the divine plan, and to the grace of the present moment, seeking neither more nor less than what God wants for it. A will that allows itself to be dethroned, and puts up no fight against its rebellious servants, is weak and does not merit the name of will, nor of good. It is not enough not to will evil.

When we give God our will fully, little by little he takes the rest, all our faculties, the whole person. The conquest no longer rests with us, but with God; it becomes his affair. As he wishes and when he wishes, he will take our memory, our senses, our passions, our imagination, intellect and heart, and he does this by the various states through which we have to pass, and by the trials he sends us. We must co-operate with him with our will in each of his loving assaults, by letting him take these things one by one.

When God is at work, the devil is not idle. When you try over a period to correct yourself on a particular point, do not be surprised if you have to submit to violent temptations on that very point, even to repeated falls. The important thing is never to admit that you are beaten. Fight and never give in, like a good general. The effort, which *is* part of the battle, even when there is nothing to show for it, plays an enormous part in the formation of the will. We always emerge from the battle stronger.

'Unless the grain of wheat dies'

∽

WHEN WE PERCEIVE THAT WE HAVE NOT BEEN attentive in prayer, that we have not been generous or recollected, and then some text of Scripture gives us fresh inspiration, or a truth appears to us in a new light, we need look no farther. This is not our work: it is the work of the Holy Spirit. That is what the inspirations of the inner life consist of, and we have no need to look elsewhere, but by a living faith seek beyond for the cause of these inspirations.

Unless the grain of wheat dies it shall not bring forth fruit. In dying, it loses its husk—a mere nothing. And at the same time, it receives all the energy of the soil to make it grow. The 'I' is the nothing that must be broken if we are to share in the divine energy; if we are to draw without measure from the divine treasury, in order that God's strength may become ours. Only thus is growth possible, but, then, what a vivifying and boundless growth!

∽∾

GOD IS THE PLENITUDE OF BEING: *I AM WHO AM*. That is how he is defined in the Old Testament. The New Testament is more precise: that Being is Love; *God is Love*. His love is co-extensive with his being: that is to say, it includes everything. To be logical, therefore, our life consists in returning in everything to that Being who is Love. This return can always be more rapid, more profound, more entire. This is the life of faith.

God is there. He leads us even when we do not see or feel his action; that lies below the surface, in the depths. We may take it that all that does not come from nature—which was 'bent' at the Fall—comes from God present in the soul, which is his image. And we may take as coming from him the movements of which we do not perceive the natural motives for acting. Our part is to detach ourselves from all these attachments, big or little, which hold us bound to persons and things, and above all to ourselves, so that we can be free to be guided by God.

But remember, what comes from the Holy Spirit, or from nature, is not yet 'ours'. What makes them ours is the acceptance by the will; it is only then that our responsibility begins.

'His place is in peace'

WHERE THERE IS PEACE, THERE IS GOD . . .
When I am calm: that is, when I leave all things
for God, at least with my will, and hold myself in
peace, all is well. It is this state which draws God.
It is a cry to God, a cry which he has been waiting
from all eternity to hear in order that he may come
and dwell in me.

And it is he himself who, by his grace, has
formed that cry in me.

Calm

∽∽

PLACE YOURSELF AS MUCH AS POSSIBLE IN THE presence of the God of love, and be calm so that you can receive his impressions. Any kind of anxiety distorts the mirror of our soul, and it no longer records God's action. Calm allows us to occupy ourselves with what we have to do without becoming preoccupied. Our intentions are directed to God, and we keep in touch with him whilst all the time doing whatever we have to do.

Yet to detach oneself for the sake of being detached, or in order to get away from creatures, is of very little value. That is Stoicism. What we have to do is to turn back to God; it is this that is so important. This should be our constant aim. We leave creatures solely because they can be an obstacle between us and God.

Never argue with yourself, with temptations. That would only be a waste of time which should be given to God. So, too, the devil can beguile us into making minute and useless examinations of conscience, which only means turning back to ourselves. It is enough, with regard to creatures, to see if they have any hold on us. If they have, turn at once back to God. Make positive acts of love: that is the great point; that is what we must do.

The inner life

∽∾

LIFE HAS AN INNER SOURCE, NAMELY GOD. AND God cannot remain inactive. It is he who gives life to all our acts. Thus our inner life is not something to be sought up in the skies, but within ourselves; not in the abstract, but in little daily happenings and acts. God is at work there, within us, with us, correcting, polishing; until—and in order that—everything in us, our faculties and their acts, are under the sway of this inner principle. We should try to reduce everything in us to this inner principle.

Hence the necessity for self-correction, the control of ourselves from within, with God's help. The virtues keep all our acts 'ordered'—towards God, our neighbour and ourselves. This is the Christian life. The 'gifts' of the Holy Spirit guide us directly; they have a direct effect; they are a higher organism which takes over as soon as all has been co-ordinated for God, and he can then do his work without encountering any obstacles in us. His least commandments are carried out, down to the tiniest fibres of our being. This is the mystical life; henceforth we have only to follow the Holy Spirit.

Simplicity is thus achieved in fact, but it presupposes a complete mastery of nature. God is the

Master-musician; the instrument no longer intro-
duces a discordant note into God's harmony.

Generosity

❧

DO NOT THINK OF GOD'S ACTION AS SOMETHING extraordinary. On the contrary, it makes itself felt in the tiny practical inspirations of every day: do this, give up that, and so on . . . Live thus, knowing that you are not alone; examine yourself in his presence, under his gaze, and be assured that he will not fail you in the least of the day's happenings. *Even [a woman] may forget her nursing child, yet I will not forget you.*

Examine yourself as regards generosity. Do you do things by half measures? Do you give yourself only half way—with God in prayer; with your neighbour in charity? Nature does its hardest to prevent us and keep us back repeatedly, and that in two ways. First, by introducing the natural spirit into all we do—by vanity, self-love—and then, negatively, by keeping back a part of the whole which of right belongs to God.

Seek God in your acts

✀

SEEK GOD IN YOUR ACTS, SINCE HE IS BEHIND them all, and we are sanctified by the acts he wants from us. Do not seek him in your ideas, by an effort of the head, but only where he is—for you. We so often seek him where he is not, and naturally we do not find him. Thus, when you are tired, for example, do not try to think things out, by abstracting from the present moment. Seek him in the tiredness itself, by accepting whole-heartedly the situation as it is. God is there; he wants just that, and that is enough.

It is the same with difficulties, with feelings of helplessness and the like. Otherwise, you will be making huge efforts, and you will accomplish nothing.

And thus everything becomes an occasion for progress: everything becomes living—and lived— a full, inner life.

God's action

༄༅

IF WE DO WHAT GOD WANTS OF US QUIETLY and with detachment, whether it be studying or reading, we may be sure that that will be quite sufficient. Given these conditions, a mere word, a few lines, can lead in our prayer later on to a repercussion more profound under God's action than the whole book read through simply as a matter of course.

Preparation

∽∾

TRUE UNDERSTANDING DOES NOT CONSIST IN the amount of matter we get through, as, for example, for an examination, but in the higher light that the intellect projects on this mass of ideas in order to co-ordinate them. Only thus will the light shine from within them, and we are able to grasp their implications. Generally speaking, the amount of knowledge we acquire is sufficient; what is more important is to make our own synthesis of this knowledge, to work personally on the material we have collected so as to make it our own. It is extraordinary how comparatively little really great people read; already understanding much, as a rule a glance is sufficient for them.

Real sanctity consists in ecstasy in the strict sense of the word: that is, in the effort of the will by which we 'go out' of ourselves in order to enter into God. It is not just settling down to take pleasure in our own particular idea of God.

On the other hand, there is great danger in the beginning for anyone who tries to plunge immediately into God, without first having made the preliminary work of preparation. We imagine we have arrived at the end, before we have even begun.

Progress

∽∾

WHAT DOES PROGRESS MEAN? PROGRESS MEANS
diligence, application and discretion. More, it
means concentration to its depths on the work we
are doing—for that is where God is for us—
without worrying about the past or the future.
That is the only way to banish all tension, all
anxiety, all those useless imaginations which are
so much more tiring than the work itself.

There are two dispositions you must never lose
sight of if you would make progress and at the
same time remain at peace. For the moment, be
content with what you are, and you will find joy
and peace, since you already possess God,
although maybe imperfectly. Bear with yourself as
you are; give simply, but fully, what you have.

As regards the future, never say: 'What I am
today is good enough for tomorrow'. Strive always
to become better; to advance towards a closer
union with God. Let the present serve as a starting
point for the future. Thus you will go from God
to God.

Life progresses slowly, and it is only what
endures that counts.

The secret of peace

ᔔᔕ

THIS IS THE SECRET OF PEACE, AFTER COM-
mitting a fault. What is past is past. And if we
accept the consequences, while bracing our will,
we can be sure that God will know how to draw
glory even from our faults. Not to be downcast
after committing a fault is one of the marks of true
sanctity, for the saint knows how to find God in
everything, in spite of human appearances. Once
your will is sincerely 'good', then *don't worry*.

True simplicity

∽∾

TAKING THINGS AS THEY ARE, IN THEMSELVES, one must everywhere and always keep oneself within bounds, since everything in human nature is limited. We are bound, therefore, to choose one thing amongst many, and at the same time put aside the others and renounce them. When, on the other hand, we cling solely to the will of God, we need never limit ourselves, because we are sharing in the plenitude of God, as also in his eternity at that moment. In things which are of themselves transitory and confined, we find what is eternal, boundless and infinite. In God we have everything in a supereminent manner. If we must limit ourselves materially, for example when we have to do a particular task, we need not do so spiritually, for by accepting the task as part of God's plan for us, we enter fully into that plan, which is something absolute and unchangeable.

This is true simplicity. In all you do, then, attach yourself to God alone, for in him you will find everything. The saints were—and are—eminently simple.

God's plan

IT IS WITHIN THE SCOPE OF GOD'S PLAN THAT we should come up against evil in this world, and have to fight a way for ourselves through it. Our Lord could have captivated the minds and hearts of the whole world by a single sermon, but he did not. Alone, with a few faithful disciples, he lived in the midst of constant hostility. It is so in the whole history of humanity—the insignificant Jewish race among the great pagan nations; the small number of the saints . . . It is the only explanation of the state of the world.

If we feel that it is beyond us to understand this, we have only to recall the divine words: *Your ways are not my ways*; and those of St Paul: *O the depth of the riches and wisdom and knowledge of God! . . . how unsearchable his ways!* We must face reality, and not live in an unreal world, not even in an ideal world of our own imagining, which we build up with our poor and unsubstantial dreams. We make a great act of adoration and submission when we recognize the absolute sovereignty of God in all that happens. Only such a thought can enable us to put up with the numberless abuses which surround us—in ourselves and others, in the Church and in the world at large.

On the practical plane, do not rush your

decisions, lest you spoil God's plan by substituting your own way of looking at things for his. If, on any particular point, circumstances indicate a change which would seem to be advisable and is feasible, act on it; but if, for various reasons, you are unable to carry it out, even though it appears to you to be desirable, then submit to the divine plan which, through the very impossibility of acting otherwise, lets us understand that God wants to tolerate the disorder for the present. Wait for God's hour. God's patience is more than we shall ever understand. He could break the resistance of all evildoers, and make all evil cease in an instant, but he does not. Adjust, then, your pace to his. Do not destroy without considering the consequences. This thought flings us back on God, and makes us pass beyond all created things.

We should try always to keep ourselves in the divine plan: that is, superior to things taken in themselves; and be glad that God has given us the opportunity to break our own will and so turn to him. This is the best way to learn to live the life of the spirit. Following Our Lord's example, we should remain steadfast in God, and regard everything as part of his plan. This is the only way to gain complete independence of created things. *He became obedient to the point of death—even death on a cross.* He trod under foot all that was purely of the senses. He dominated it all completely, and thus entered into his glory. Everything human was crushed so that God might be exalted on its ruins.

We must not be surprised if, while the cross lasts, we experience no feeling of elevation or consolation; that, on the contrary, we are often incapable of raising up our spirits or of thinking of the good effects which will follow later. More often than not, all we can do at the moment is to accept and offer up our distress to Our Lord.

Contemplation

CONTEMPLATION IS NOTHING MORE THAN A constant, loving, looking at God. Exteriorly, the life of a contemplative is like that of any other person. There is no need to imagine states which would necessitate a change of condition. A contemplative is subject to the same difficulties, the same troubles, the same anxieties, discouragements, feelings of helplessness, imperfections and even faults, as anyone else. The great point is that in all things the contemplative knows how to find God, for he goes to the heart of things. For him, the veil represented by the creature is raised just a little, and he sees only the love of God in everything. Hence his peace after committing a fault.

To arrive at such a state one must endeavour not to stop at the thing itself, nor to let oneself become too absorbed by it, but pass beyond it by a loving faith. We should make a habit of seeing God in everything. Our occupations must not— they should not—mean more to us than they are: that is to say, just means. We must accept them, take delight in them, only in so far as they come from God, and lead us back to him. God gives us the means to sanctify ourselves by everything, but above all by those things which are contrary to our nature and our tastes.

Contemplation is the disposition of being all for God; receiving everything from him, allowing him to act in us, overcoming all difficulties which are opposed to his action. For the divine action is far higher than that of the highest of our human faculties. Already in this life it is an end; everything else constitutes the means. Even the highest theological speculation remains in the category of means. Our ideal is to know how to co-ordinate everything by the total gift of self, towards direct union with God.

Finally, contemplation is the plenitude of God in the present moment. It is receiving moment by moment the full action of God, who gives himself to us continuously.

Live on God's level

∾

IN ALL THAT WE DO, AND AT EVERY MOMENT, God has ordained an exact balance between what we have to do and the necessary strength to do it; and this we call grace. Our part is to bring ourselves into line with grace.

God uses all the horrors of this world for an infinitely perfect end, and always with an infinite calm. It is part of his plan that we should feel the blows and experience the wounds of life; but more than anything else he wants us to dominate them by the virtues of faith, hope and charity, and so live on his level. It is these latter which will raise us up to him, and then we shall share in his calm, in the highest part of our being.

Allow God to act

❧

OUR BUSINESS IN LIFE CONSISTS SOLELY IN keeping ourselves in the dispositions which allow God to act. There will surely be progress so long as we do not put our spoke in God's wheels, as the saying is, in order to have our own way.

Love is the sole standard where God is concerned. Provided we come back to him, the past is entirely blotted out. A great sinner who by contrition and penance has arrived at the same degree of love as a just man, has exactly the same value in God's sight. This is the meaning of the Redemption, which makes the marred work of creation even more beautiful than it was before. To think otherwise would be to lessen the work of Christ. At the foot of the Cross St John stood on one side, St Mary Magdalen on the other—on the same level!

Carrying our cross

❧

OUR LORD CARRIED HIS CROSS, AND WE MUST carry ours: that is, the tiny, daily crosses proportioned to our weakness. That is how we prove our love for his Cross, by uniting ours to his; and it is this that gives ours the merit of his Cross.

In order to bear our crosses, we must always have recourse to the thought that this is how God wants things for us, and say to ourselves: 'I have him who is my All, and that is enough for me'. I must be indifferent to and independent of everything else . . .

We must never say that that kind of sanctity—forgetfulness of self, love of the Cross, self-immolation and so on—are not for us. That is our human way of looking at things. If God wants them of us, he will send the necessary graces; all we must do is to hold ourselves in readiness for anything that he may ask of us, and go ahead fearlessly.

Steady effort

❧

SPASMODIC EFFORTS AT MAKING PROGRESS ARE
A sign of weakness, rather than otherwise. What
we need is steady effort; not constrained, but calm
like a river moving quietly on its course. Think
of the majesty of the ordered movement of the
stars . . .

Life is adaptation

〜〜

LIFE IS ADAPTATION: THAT IS, FINDING JOY IN everything, passing above everything, trusting wholly in God. *I can do all things through him.* Nothing can resist that. Take a lesson from the plants, which never cease to develop, bending themselves to the inclemency of the weather, growing continuously, profiting from all the varying circumstances of weather and soil. To arrive at our goal, we would like to have a straight line marked out for us, all plain sailing, as though life were a map. But life is not like that. It is a divine plan, which has to carve a way for itself through all sorts of undergrowth—by hills and valleys, following the difficulties of the way, tunnels, hills and detours—that is life; all so long as we do not stop. Therefore, look things in the face, and adapt yourself to them day by day. The changes of season, the succession of heat and cold, sun and rain, day and night: all these things contribute, do they not, to the ripening of the fruit? So it is with the soul.

There is order in reason, and another order in life. Reason divides, classifies, co-ordinates, mechanically. Life on the other hand is a synthesis, and cannot be explained by reason. For instance, we take a rose to pieces to see what it is, and what there is in it. With what result? We have all the parts that compose the rose, but we no longer have a living rose.

We may—and should—use our imagination and reason to form in us an intuitive intellect. They are good and necessary, as in theology for instance, in order that we may understand and contemplate truth under all its aspects. But we still have to make our own synthesis, at once vital and living. Take for example the attributes of God. It is not enough to consider them in theory, speculatively; they must be made to enter into our lives, into our very being. By our reason we obtain fresh light on our concepts, but it is by faith that we respond to life, because it is the life of faith which puts us in touch with God, as he is in himself, not as he exists in our abstract knowledge of him. Faith enables us to grasp life as a whole, moment by moment; by faith we rise above all that we see or understand or feel, and touch directly the living God, who cannot be attained by reason. There you have the difference between the erudition of a scholar and the life of a saint.

Natural inclinations

ᘡᘡ

THE ONLY WAY TO DEAL WITH OUR NATURAL inclinations is to go to the root of the matter: that is, transform them by contrary acts. We must do bravely what we do not like doing; keep a tight rein on the things that give us pleasure. The simple, indeed the indispensable and infallible, means to take them in hand is to recall the words of the Gospel: *If any want to become my followers, let them deny themselves . . .*

Grace perfects nature, and where nature is deficient, grace makes up for what is wanting. But, if we are to attain to perfection, it must do more than that: it must go against our natural tendencies and transform them. That is why, in tending to perfection, men must exercise and cultivate the feminine virtues of kindness, devotedness, patience and gentleness, since these are the difficult ones for them to acquire. Women, on the other hand, need the male virtues of courage, energy and justice. Then, after a number of years, as we begin to grow old, the final perfection in both cases will consist in a spiritual childhood, in which we must react against the defects of nature which by that time has been formed and wants to assert itself: for example, by imposing one's personality, by pride and the desire to command.

111

Grace

೦ಌ೦

As grace is grafted on to nature, and does
not supplant it, one of the best ways, together with
prayer, of drawing down grace is to endeavour to
dispose our nature to receive grace, to render it
capable of receiving it to advantage. For grace
respects God's order, and will only act on a nature
already well disposed. We 'dispose' it by forming
habits, and this we do by repeated acts. The soil
is then ready to receive the action of grace with
profit. Grace of itself will always do its work; it is
we who have the power to spoil its action, just as
a badly tuned instrument, played by however so
fine an artist, cannot render a melody har-
moniously.

Difficulties, upsets, struggles and the like are
our greatest blessings here and now, and we should
thank God specially for them, for it is above all by
them that he forms us, indeed transforms us.
These trials are a necessary part of our training in
this life, if we are to achieve our end in the life to
come.

This transformation in God must extend to all
our faculties. These, directed by the will, must
take the same direction—towards the Father, each
sustaining the other, and tending with all their
combined strength towards God: in the case of the

mind by nourishing it with concepts of faith; in the case of the will by making it follow these concepts in order to dominate our lower nature.

This we do by remembering that our only real strength is our spiritual strength. It is hopeless to attempt to combat our sensitive impressions directly: that would be to fight a losing battle. Our only hope of victory is to take refuge in the higher part of the soul and remain there in calm and peace, letting the lower parts carry on their clamour, but without allowing them in the least to upset or trouble us. We must not be surprised at these apparent contradictions. We must face life as we find it, and as God permits it in our regard. Whatever we do, we must not nourish ourselves on dreams and illusions.

Impressions

❧

IN THE MIDST OF LIFE'S CONTINUOUS DISTUR-
bances, both within and without us, we must
reflect on the unchangeableness of God and rest
therein. We do this, above all, by an activity which
is co-ordinated, controlled and constant; by trying
to cultivate an equal, steady movement in all that
we do, by avoiding too violent enthusiasms with
their consequent depressions, by paying no attention to our impressions and feelings, which are
movements we cannot control. Whatever life
brings, we can always try to bear it or undertake
it for God's sake. The one thing he asks of us is
to keep our will turned towards him, no matter
what our present state may be. Impressions and
results do not depend upon our will, and should
not stop us, or even interest us. We have a certain
task to perform. Then we must do it as well as we
can, for the love of God, and leave the rest entirely
to him. We must keep an even keel, in both our
will and intention, in spite of our sensitive reactions. This is so important if God is to act. In that
way, one is always at his disposition. We lose no
time looking at ourselves, gazing backwards or for-
wards. If we fail in anything, we must turn back
immediately to God, and carry on. Only one thing
we must not do, and that is, refuse God anything

he asks of us, for then there is no longer union of will and he cannot act in us. But to work when we are not feeling like it or without finding any pleasure in it; not to be able to pray as we would like—these are not obstacles to God's action, provided the will takes hold of them as it finds them, and offers them up to God.

We must not be surprised, then, or disturbed at the unsatisfactoriness or shortcomings of God's creatures: it is all in his plan. It is not our complete perfection that makes something of us, or that God wants of us, but that we should reflect something of his infinite perfection, each according to his capacity. To expect absolute perfection of everyone is impossible and would be to live in an unreal world. Everyone has but a tiny place in the Mystical Body; nevertheless, we each contribute in our measure to the perfection of the whole.

Festina lente

∽∾

THERE ARE SOME PEOPLE WHO ACT ON THEIR ideas at once, but in general they do not see far or go far. Their horizons remain bounded by their too rapid realization of things. They arrive at a certain result, and then stop. Others, on the other hand, spend a long time thinking and meditating before they act. These, I think one can say, go farther if more slowly. It is a question of temperament, and we must not let ourselves be worried by their slowness. For God, whatever is 'natural'—whatever does not depend upon our will—is never an obstacle. It is our faults, not our defects, which hinder the work of grace.

The meaning of the Incarnation

〜∽〜

INSTEAD OF ATTEMPTING TO FREE OURSELVES from the things of the senses, or abstracting from them, we should try to probe deeper into them; not stopping at their external appearance, which changes, but seeking what is hidden deep in their substance: their being, in a word. For God is Being. And thus we shall find him beneath the veil of the senses.

This is the meaning of the Incarnation. God became tangible, in order to teach us to find him in all that we touch and see and feel; for we are necessarily bound to the senses in this life. Jesus did not do away with these external contacts; what he taught us is not to stop at them. He taught us to find his Father in everything: in the flowers, in the lilies of the field, in the birds, in sorrow— in everything, because everything comes from his love, and must return to it. *In him we see our God made visible, and so are caught up in the love of the God we cannot see.**

We must endeavour, therefore, to cultivate this spiritual 'second-sight'. It is the secret of the saints, for whom this world is not an obstacle

---

*Preface of Christmas: *ut dum visibiliter Deum cognoscimus, per hunc in invisibilium amorem rapiamur.*

between their souls and God, but a living image, a resplendent mirror of his goodness and beauty. It is this great Reality, so utterly beyond our conception, that the Incarnation made possible: that by loving and imitating Jesus incarnate, we love and imitate God himself.

Our inner life

❧

OUR INNER LIFE SHOULD BE JUDGED BY OUR reactions to difficulties, obstacles, the shocks that we meet with in life, not by fanciful theories. The life around us wounds our sensitive nature; but our inner life reacts by finding its support in reason and faith, in the consideration of the true value of things, in the thought of eternity. Those who have nothing more than their sensitive nature to fall back on are bound to be superficial. And when their sensitiveness is broken, shaken and tossed about, their whole being is carried away by the current; they no longer have anything solid to hold on to.

What is the real effect of all our external activities on our deep interior life; on our real advancement? We cannot tell, for that is the exclusive work of the Holy Spirit, who is the sole Source of our spiritual life. In the end, it is grace which touches the heart.

Enthusiasms

∾∾

To be united to our idea of God and united to God are two very different things. In the one case, we remain in ourselves, and that is egoism; in the other, we go out of ourselves in order to find God; to find ourselves again in him. People with philosophical minds can pass the whole of their lives contemplating their idea of God, without ever crossing the threshold of experimental union with him: a union intimate, profound, direct and lived. We should always be on our guard against such an illusion. There are some people who think they have arrived, and remain in that illusion, when they have not even started. Watch your enthusiasms, both in yourself and in others, above all in the beginning.

As regards meditation: books and methods are only means for uniting ourselves to God. They are not an occupation or end in themselves. Prayer is not so much the time to try to get to the bottom of an idea, as to place ourselves in God's presence in a manner at once living and lived, a going-out from oneself. With such a basic disposition, everything is good and can serve our purpose. The best method, always assuming one feels drawn to it, is to remain faithfully in the presence of God, dismissing by an act of the will all that is not

God. Keep repeating: 'My God and my All', or some such thought, which will always bring you back to him as to your centre. If you can do this, do not bother about anything else.

Defects

∾∾

DEFECTS ARE NEVER A DANGER, PROVIDED WE are aware of them, and take them in hand. The danger is rather in not facing them, or in wanting to pass them over without bothering about them. It is a delusion to want to press forward to new conquests, before we have overcome the enemies behind us.

God asks of us all that we have, nothing more. That is why we must not look at what we give God, because often we have nothing to give him, or practically nothing. Sometimes we have only our misery to offer him; but he does not mind, so long as we refuse him nothing.

Criticism

∽∾

IN THE MATTER OF CRITICISM, ONE CAN SAY IN general that where it is a question of speaking of a fact, we are simply making a statement. When one is speaking of a person, however, or expressing an opinion on the fact, then one is making a judgement. The fact itself can be capable of either a good or bad interpretation, but beyond that one should not go. For nearly always we are ignorant of the intention, the responsibility, the circumstances of the case—often almost entirely, always in part. Every question, every fact, considered under all its aspects, is so to say of infinite complexity. There are situations in which one has to judge persons by what one sees: this is the case of those who have charge of others, or who have to make decisions. But even then, one must leave the final judgement to God.

Apart from such cases, one should abstain from judging as much as possible.

Trust in God

∽∾

TRUST IN GOD WITH AN ABSOLUTE, UNBOUNDED
trust, independent of your feelings or state of
mind. Remember St Paul's: *Scio enim cui
credidi . . . I know the one in whom I have put my
trust.* Examine yourself on this point of filial
relationship. See where you fail, or what could
interfere with it. Our want of trust is only bad
when it is wilful. If the will is good, you will win
through in the end, for it is God who is at work.
In order to have full and constant confidence in
God, however, in your fundamental relations with
him and so correspond fully at every moment, you
must become more and more master of your acts.
Try always to perform human, that is conscious
acts. There is no sin in not doing so, but conscious acts give God so much more glory, and
they dispose us to receive more grace. In order
to acquire the habit of making controlled acts,
therefore, we should endeavour to do everything
calmly, a little at a time but steadily, in the beginning even somewhat slowly. We should not speak
without knowing clearly what we want to say; com-
pleting our sentences and avoiding all stock
phrases, repetitions, useless expressions and the
like. In a word, we must try to act always like one
who knows what he wants, and where he is going.

Do not let matters which belong to reason, such as decisions, appreciations and judgements, slip back into sentiment. That is to say, do not let yourself be moved or upset by matters which should be considered calmly. We should get into the habit of keeping our inner life proof against all that is on the outside. We must not let these things 'nag' at us: it is this which is so tiring, the constant struggle against the tyranny of our feelings, once we allow them to get inside us and remain there, for then they fight against our convictions. We must try to acquire the habit of being guided by an act of the mind, which takes a simple view of things, of the facts, and which does not tire. Watch the combatants, but do not go down yourself into the arena. Watch them from above: examine that is to say, but impartially, the passions which, when they get the upper hand, upset and falsify the judgement.

As regards yourself, treat yourself as you would others. Look at yourself from above, and do not let yourself be moved by either emotion or self-pity for your poor wounds. In short, live as in eternity, concern yourself with the substance of things, with your relations with God. But do not allow the 'accidents' of your acts to spoil the serenity of your soul, which should be given entirely to God.

Resolutions

‿◠‿

MAKE FIRM RESOLUTIONS, PRECISE AND SUITED to your state: little at a time and practical, so that you will not be discouraged if you are not able to keep them. Then, never argue about them, especially when the time comes for action. In the same way, never make decisions when you are under any kind of emotion, or when your sensitiveness might falsify your judgement: wait until you are calm.

Remember the Latin tag: *Age quod agis* . . . do what you are doing. Give yourself wholly to what you have in hand. It is this that makes the man. Do not do things by halves; do not dissipate your strength, but bring the whole of your energy to bear on the duty of the moment. You will find the result will be increased ten-fold.

It is this which also makes the Christian, provided that in everything we realize as much as possible our duty for God's sake. In so doing, we will *run in the way of the commandments*; not only so, but we will run more steadily, because each moment will be a full moment: we will experience those 'full days' spoken of by the Psalmist.*

*Cf. Ps. 72: 10 (Vulgate): *Therefore will my people return here: and full days shall be found in them.*

That is the way to acquire perseverance and strength; to avoid making vain and futile efforts, hesitating indecisions, all the things that tire us most, even physically. For we are then like an engine, running free, out of gear. Nothing helps to maintain our moral equilibrium so much as a regular and rational development, with everything ordered towards a definite object.

God and the world

∽∾

IN THE MIDST OF ALL THE HORRORS, ATROCITIES and crimes which are being committed in the world, God sees only his Son. He gave him to the world: an immense, infinite proof of his love. *God so loved the world, that he gave his only Son.* The Word passes down the centuries, radiating light and love. *He was the true light that enlightens everyone coming into the world,* inviting everyone to come and be united to him. *He gave [them] power to become children of God.* God sees only this well-beloved Son, and those who in receiving him become his living image, his reproduction. The world exists for no other purpose than this.

God does not force us to come to him, for then love would not be the true motive. There must be a loving response on our part. Some accept him, and then God loves them in his Son. United to him, they become one with him, and the Father looks upon them both with a single regard of delight. Others refuse him, and God seems to leave them to themselves, to what they have chosen, to follow their own way, as if he no longer looked upon them: but only as long as their refusal is obstinate and persistent, for he calls to everyone again and again.

Two loves and two planes

⌘

THERE ARE TWO KINDS OF LOVE; OR, RATHER, two forms of the same love: that of God and of our neighbour. But we arrive at them in different ways.

The first we achieve by knowing as much as we can of God, who is the object of our love; by studying him both in himself and in his works. This is because he is infinitely good, and all knowledge of him draws us to him.

The second, the love of our neighbour, we arrive at in a contrary manner: by not knowing too much about him, by making excuses for him, by not scrutinizing him too closely, by covering up his faults. This is because human beings are not perfect, and we can only love one another by regarding one another in God, or God in us.

So, too, there are two planes, and we should not allow the lower to intrude into the higher. We can be aware of the defects of others, but we should not allow these defects to stir up our feelings or passions. It is the same with, for example, an act of charity. We should not spoil it by showing personal feelings or antipathy. Our higher life should be strong enough to dominate and carry with it the lower life, at least to a great extent. For there will always be times when we cannot help being annoyed by absurd little things. But when that happens, we should try to supernaturalize them by accepting them and offering them to God.

Prayer

ເບຣ

ALWAYS BEGIN WITH AN ACT OF THE PRESENCE of God. This is an act of faith in Divine Love: living, present, loving, looking at us, coming to our aid, keeping us ever aware of his action. We must look at him as we would at a Father, and speak to him accordingly. So long as we have not retracted that act—that is, so long as we have not made a contrary act or one that would imply anything to the contrary—the force of our act of faith at the beginning of our prayer persists, and every time we put away a disturbing thought we renew it.

Our greatest obstacle is when we look at ourselves. We want to know what we are doing, how we stand; but we must do just the opposite. We must make the effort to forget ourselves.

Then, too, we must not be afraid to do all our spiritual exercises with our whole being. *Os, lingua, mens, sensus, vigor . . .* * God wants our faith in his

Translator's note: The reference is to the second verse of the Hymn at Terce of the Day:

> Let flesh and heart and lips and mind
> Sound forth our witness to mankind;
> And love light up our mortal frame,
> Till others catch the living flame.

love to be a full and virile act. Never mind if it does not move the emotions: that is God's part. But if it does, so much the better.

Fidelity

꩜

LIVE CALMLY ACCORDING TO THE LIGHTS YOU have received during your time of recollection and prayer. They are the seeds God has given you in order that they may develop. Henceforth he will give you day by day the graces necessary for their development. These graces will not probably sanctify you as you would like, but if you are faithful they will sanctify you as he likes, and that is the real sanctity.

Fidelity does not consist in not falling, nor in arriving at perfection all at once. That is the fidelity we shall possess in heaven. On earth, it consists in the will which makes us get up again repeatedly, in spite of our imperfections and falls. It does this, because that is how God wants it, and he will always give us the necessary strength. Patience with others, and confidence in God: let that be our watchword. *Do this, and you will live.*

Biblical references in the text

∽∾

References to the Psalms are numbered according to the Vulgate Version. Most biblical quotations in the text are given in the New Revised Standard Version of the Bible, except where the sense given by the Vulgate and its translation is that required by the author.

134